# AWESOME
## Construction Activities
## for Kids

# AWESOME CONSTRUCTION ACTIVITIES for Kids

## 25 S T E A M

### CONSTRUCTION PROJECTS TO DESIGN AND BUILD

AKYIAA MORRISON, PE

ROCKRIDGE
PRESS

For general information on our other products and services or to obtain technical support, please contact our Customer Care Department within the United States at (866) 744-2665, or outside the United States at (510) 253-0500.

Rockridge Press publishes its books in a variety of electronic and print formats. Some content that appears in print may not be available in electronic books, and vice versa.

Series Designer: Katy Brown
Interior and Cover Designer: Richard Tapp
Art Producer: Tom Hood
Editor: Mary Colgan
Production Editor: Matthew Burnett
Production Manager: Michael Kay

Illustrations © Kate Francis, 2021. Photography © Andrew Purcell, 2021, cover; zorandimzr/iStock, p. ii; Teen00000/Dreamstime.com, p. vi; kate_sept2004/Istock, p. viii; Shutterstock, p. x; Elnur/Dreamstime.com, p. 14; Anutr Yossundara/Dreamstime.com, p. 96.

Paperback ISBN: 978-1-63807-452-6
eBook ISBN: 978-1-63807-189-1

R0

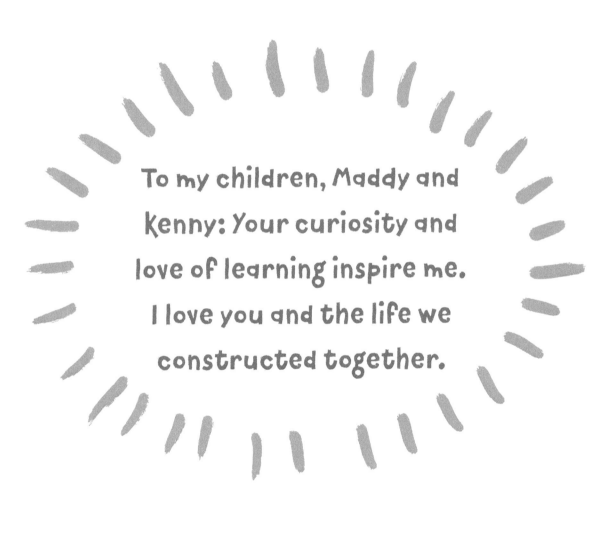

To my children, Maddy and Kenny: Your curiosity and love of learning inspire me. I love you and the life we constructed together.

# CONTENTS

# INTRODUCTION

Welcome to *Awesome Construction Activities*! This book was made especially for kids who are crazy about construction. If you get excited driving by construction sites, you're going to love diving into each of the book's 25 projects based on different aspects of the construction process.

As a little girl growing up in Trinidad and Tobago, I remember driving under a new bridge that was under construction. There were always engineers on site, looking over plans and coordinating work. From that moment, I knew I wanted to work in construction. Today, as a registered Professional Engineer and a proud homeschooling parent, I am passionate about education and getting children excited about engineering. I believe that every child, regardless of background, deserves to have their passions supported and encouraged. Any child from anywhere can grow up to become an engineer, and that includes you!

Just like real construction projects, the activities in this book will get a little messy!

Find one area that will be your project site. This is where you will build all of your projects! There are also a few key materials that you'll need for some of your projects. Try to gather everything you need together on the project site. Most materials are household items or can easily be bought at a dollar store.

Each activity outlines how it relates to real life, provides simple and easy-to-understand concepts about how and why we do each project, and points out a STEAM connection that links the different aspects of STEAM to the project.

This book shares a real-life engineer's perspective on everything that is important about construction. Through each activity, you can fuel your passion for construction and learn some things that you may not have realized before, especially about construction sites.

Get ready to dive into the exciting world of construction!

### Part 1

# DESIGN AND BUILD

**Do you like building train tracks or stacking** blocks as tall as you can before they fall over? These are STEAM activities! Building things like these is fun and exciting, but we are also learning all about what it means to be an engineer! Engineers use STEAM every day. STEAM stands for science, technology, engineering, art, and math. It is an important part of how we solve problems to improve our lives.

**S T E A M** is also a big part of construction. But what exactly is construction? How does it begin? Who plans and designs the projects? How do they do so? And what skills are needed to complete construction projects? You'll learn the answers to these questions in this section.

# Chapter One

# WHAT IS CONSTRUCTION?

**Have you ever driven past a construction site** and wondered what they were doing? Construction is the process of building **infrastructure**. Infrastructure is anything that we build that supports modern life. Bridges, buildings, tunnels, railroads, highways, and even water treatment facilities are all examples of infrastructure.

Engineers use different types of equipment during construction to make their work easier. Bulldozers push dirt, excavators dig, and dump trucks haul things away. Construction sites are usually full of dust and dirt, but sometimes we have to get a little dirty before we can create something truly awesome, and that's what construction is all about!

This chapter will help you understand more about what construction is, the different types of engineers that design and build infrastructure, what those engineers actually do, and how you can become a part of the world of construction, both now and in the future.

# THE FIRST JOB SITES

Engineers have been designing and building infrastructure since the earliest days of civilization. People built huts and shelters to protect themselves from bad weather and predators. Over time, as they learned how to use better building materials and found new ways of building things, they started to design and build more complex infrastructure.

The Egyptian pyramids were built over 4,000 years ago to be used as burial places and monuments. The Egyptians realized that they could use the Nile River to transport the blocks they needed for building. Just as engineers use heavy equipment on modern construction sites to make their jobs easier, the Egyptians figured out how to make transporting the blocks to the site easier!

The ancient Romans built huge channels, or aqueducts, to supply fresh water to their cities. These aqueducts transported water from as far as 60 miles away! They figured out how to design the aqueducts just right. If they were too steep, the force of the water would wear away the surface, but if they were too shallow, then the water couldn't flow properly. Because of these aqueducts, the Romans showed how it was possible to have a civilization away from a water source.

Engineers today have learned from all the improvements that have been made over time. They always look for ways to make the design and build processes even better. Today, thanks to civil and construction engineers, we have skyscrapers, smooth roads to drive on, clean water to drink, and safe ways to dispose of our waste.

## What Is a Civil Engineer?

Could you imagine if you had to go to a stream every day to collect water? Could you imagine how you would get from place to place if you had no roads? Could you imagine if your house flooded every time it rained? Civil engineers design infrastructure so that we don't have to worry about any of these things.

There are many types of civil engineers, and here are some examples:

**Structural engineers** design structures like buildings and bridges. They have to make sure that these structures are strong enough to withstand all kinds of forces like earthquakes, wind, snow, and even people.

**Geotechnical engineers** look at soil and rock to design foundations that will properly support structures. They also make sure that the ground is stable enough to avoid things like landslides.

**Transportation engineers** make sure that people and goods can be easily transported from one place to another. They design things like streets, highways, railroads, subways, shipping ports, and airports.

**Environmental engineers** protect both the environment and people by designing things like water or wastewater treatment facilities. They also design landfills to dispose of waste as safely as possible.

**Water resource, or hydraulic, engineers** look at the flow of water and design channels and levees to help control flooding. They also design dams to help generate electricity.

In this book, we will work on projects that focus on each of these types of civil engineers. Civil engineers design things you can see, and many things you don't, but these things are all important to our daily lives.

## What Is a Construction Engineer?

Construction engineers take the designs that civil engineers create and make sure that the project is built exactly as it is in the design. Construction engineers work on a lot of different tasks. They make sure that projects are built on scope (built how they were designed), on time (finished when they are supposed to be), and on budget (only costing as much as planned). They design and build temporary structures to keep workers and the public safe. These will stay in place during construction but will be removed after the project is complete. They also solve any unexpected problems with the project. Construction engineers work on construction sites, and they look at the materials and construction methods that construction workers are using. They make sure that workers, the public, and the environment are safe during construction.

Construction engineers have a lot of hands-on project experience and can double-check designs to look for things that might make construction difficult. For example, they may suggest a different or new construction entrance if the existing entrance is too small for large equipment to get into. Sometimes a construction engineer might find something on a construction site that the civil engineer did not expect. For example, there may be an underground pipe that nobody knew about when the project was being designed. In cases like these, the construction engineer will work with the civil engineer to figure out the best solution to keep the project going.

## HOW DO ENGINEERS WORK?

Engineers have come up with ways to solve all kinds of problems, no matter how hard those problems might be. For an engineer to solve a problem, they must understand exactly what the problem is. Next, they try to figure out all the different ways that they can solve that problem. Once they have a list, they choose the best idea, come up with a plan, and bring that plan to life by building it. Sometimes, things don't work as the engineer thought they would. Engineers then improve the design and keep improving until everything works the way they wanted it to.

When engineers solve problems, they follow the engineering design process. As long as engineers follow all the steps in the engineering design process, they can figure out a solution to any problem. The steps of this process are:

Ask

Imagine

Plan

Create

Improve

## Ask

In this first step, engineers ask questions about the problem they are trying to solve. What is the problem? How is it different from a similar problem that has already been solved? Is there anything special to consider when coming up with a solution? Engineers must ask questions to get more details about project requirements, and they must also ask questions to see what has been done before and how they can improve on those designs.

## Imagine

Once engineers have asked questions to understand the problem that they need to solve, they must now imagine possible solutions. In a process called brainstorming, engineers think about any solutions that might work for that problem. In this step, no idea is a bad idea!

## Plan

After coming up with lots of different possible solutions, engineers must choose the best option and start to come up with a plan. Engineers can draw their designs to show how the solution would work, list the different materials they would need, and think about how much it would cost to build it.

## Create

When engineers are happy with the plans they have made, they can now follow through on their plan and build something! The create stage lets engineers jump in and see if their plans really work like they thought they would or if they need to change something.

## Improve

If the projects that they have created don't work like they thought they would, engineers can figure out how to improve them! They look closely at what worked and what didn't work so they can make their design better.

All the activities in this book will help you practice the engineering design process yourself so you can start coming up with your very own solutions to some very big problems! Can you think of any problems today that you want to solve with the help of the engineering design process?

## WHAT DO I NEED TO KNOW TO DESIGN AND BUILD?

STEAM stands for Science, Technology, Engineering, Art, and Math. Every part of STEAM is used in construction and every part is important. What would happen if math weren't used to take measurements and a house ended up being built on top of a sidewalk? Or what if art wasn't used as a house was being designed, so one of the windows ended up facing a brick wall? This is why civil and construction engineers must use every part of STEAM to successfully design and build their projects. They must also be able to work as part of a team and ask for help if they need it.

Civil and construction engineers need to understand concepts from science, such as the law of gravity and how forces act on things, to make sure the structures they build are strong and safe. They use technology when they come up with designs on their computers or use machines on site. For example, if they want to locate hidden pipes underground without digging anything up, they can use special imaging machines. Art is also an important part of engineering, since engineers can design beautiful, intricate structures. Even math is used in every part of construction, like measuring angles and learning what shapes are the strongest to support a structure. Science, technology, engineering, art, and math all work together and allow engineers to design and build the infrastructure we see—or don't see—every day.

As you do the projects in this book yourself, you will learn all about why engineers do what they do as they design and build amazing things.

# Chapter Two

# HOW TO USE THIS BOOK

Race cars are fun, but have you ever thought about what it takes to build a road or a bridge for them to drive on? Have you wondered what happens when you flush the toilet? Where does the water go? How do you get clean water every time you turn on your faucet? If you have ever wondered about things like these, you are already on your way to becoming an engineer!

Engineers have curious minds and are always trying to understand how things work and how to make them better. In this book, you will follow step-by-step instructions to help you build things like railroads, bridges, construction equipment, and more. These projects will help you understand exactly how these things work so you can try to make them even better!

## GETTING READY

You can choose any project you want to do first, so start with the project that seems like the most fun to you! When you are getting ready to do your projects, make sure that you have all your materials ready before you start. Most materials are things you can find around the house, but you might need to buy some things at a store. Take some time to flip through the book, look at the materials for the projects you would like to do first, and make a list so you can get them at the same time. Each project shows the amount of time it should take to finish. Make sure you have enough time so you don't have to rush!

Each project has a small introduction that explains what the project is about. You might want to jump right into doing the activity, but make sure you read this introduction first! This will help you understand how engineers design and build things and why each project is important.

Projects can be easy, medium, or challenging. Some projects might have caution notes for safety, so make sure you have a grown-up help you with these. Try working on an easy project first, and when you get the hang of it, you can move on to a medium or challenging one!

Since these projects are about construction, things might get a little messy, and you will even have to go outside to do some of them. That's okay! Remember, in construction, sometimes you have to get a little bit dirty to build something awesome!

## DOING THE PROJECTS

After choosing your project, getting your materials ready, and getting help from a grown-up, you are ready to start! Each project has step-by-step instructions for you to follow. There are also pictures so you know what your project is supposed to look like along the way. Each picture will be labeled with a number so you know which step it's showing.

First, read through all the steps so you know what you'll have to do to finish your project. Next, complete each step; it is important that you read and follow the directions carefully. If something isn't working as you think it should, or if your project looks a little different than the pictures, don't worry! This is all part of engineering. Remember the last step in the engineering design process is to improve! If something you created doesn't work like you wanted it to, this is your chance to try again and improve it!

Some words in the book will be in **bold**. These words can be found in the glossary at the back of the book. The glossary is full of important words or terms you will need to know as a future engineer!

When you have completed your activity, be sure to check out the Hows & Whys section so you can understand how the project works in real life and why engineers need to do it! You should also read the STEAM Connection so you can understand how the different parts of STEAM are used in your project. Lastly, there is room throughout the book where you can write notes on how you can improve the project or design your very own version!

## ESSENTIAL SUPPLIES

*Although the supplies for each project may be a little different, there are some supplies that you will find yourself reaching for again and again while using this book. It will be helpful to have the following supplies ready for multiple projects:*

- *Cardboard*
- *Cardboard tubes*
- *Cardstock sheets*
- *Craft sticks*
- *Low-temperature glue gun and glue sticks*
- *Modeling clay*
- *Pebbles or gravel*
- *Sand*
- *Scissors*
- *Shoeboxes*
- *Tape*
- *White glue*

### Part II

# THE PROJECTS

**Are you ready to have fun with construction?**
You will do all kinds of construction projects, from building construction tools like augers and wheelbarrows, to even building a bridge or tower! You will learn how to build a variety of projects while using your own creativity to develop ideas and solve problems to make the results even better. Let's jump in!

# BUILD A SOIL TESTER

DIFFICULTY LEVEL: EASY
TIME: 15 MINUTES (PLUS
1 HOUR WAIT TIME)

## MATERIALS

- Glass jar with lid (any size)
- Dirt (from your yard or store-bought garden soil)
- Water
- Measuring tape

Engineers build structures in a lot of different places. They have to understand what type of soil, or dirt, is at the site to make sure that the structures they design and build are safe. Engineers have to change the way they design and build structures based on what type of soil they find. In this activity, you will learn about the different types of soil particles that are in your own backyard.

## STEPS

1. Fill the first third of your glass jar with dirt.

2. Fill the jar almost to the top with water.

3. Screw the lid onto your jar, and shake well until all the dirt and water are mixed. Shake until there are no clumps of soil left.

4. Leave your jar somewhere it will not be disturbed.

5. After one hour, take a look at your jar. You will see different layers in the dirt. Use your measuring tape to measure the height of each layer and the total height of the dirt and water.

6. Sand particles are the biggest and will be at the bottom of the jar. **Silt** particles are smaller than sand but larger than clay, so they form the next layer. Clay particles are the smallest and are on top of the silt. Water will be the next layer, and it might be a little brown because of organic matter dissolved in it. Organic solids float on top of the water. Which layer is the biggest: sand, silt, or clay? Or is there an even mix of all three?

**HOWS & WHYS:** All soil is a mixture of different particles. Soil can have sand, silt, clay, and organic material. Clay expands when wet and shrinks when dry. It does not drain very well, so soil that has a lot of clay can cause foundations to shift or even crack. Silt holds water and also does not drain very well. Silty soils can push against foundations and make them weak. Sand has large particles that allow water to drain well, but it can also be washed away. Sandy soils can sometimes leave gaps under foundations.

It is important for soil to have a good mix of clay, silt, and sand. This is called **loam**. If this is not possible, engineers can make special designs that make up for any problems that a type of soil may cause.

**STEAM CONNECTION:** You are using science to understand how different soil particles behave. Sand, silt, and clay particles are all different sizes, so they settle at different levels when mixed with water.

# BUILD A PAPER CUP TOWER

**DIFFICULTY LEVEL:** EASY
**TIME:** 20 MINUTES

## MATERIALS

- 14 (12-ounce) paper cups
- 2 (14-by-14-inch) pieces of cardboard

Do you think it's possible for a paper cup to be able to hold your weight? In this activity, you will learn the difference between **force** and **pressure** as you build your own paper cup tower!

## STEPS

1. Place two cups side by side on the ground. While holding on to a wall (or your parents) for support, try standing on the cups. Do the cups hold your weight, or do they break?

2. Arrange six cups in two rows of three cups each. Place one piece of cardboard on top of the cups. While holding on to a wall (or your parents) for support, try standing on the tower. Does it hold your weight, or does it break?

3. Repeat step 2 to add a second layer. While holding on to a wall (or your parents) for support, try standing on the tower. Does it hold your weight or does it break?

**HOWS & WHYS:** Pressure is how much force acts over an area. Whenever you make the area that a force acts on bigger, you lessen the pressure. When you first try to stand on the paper cups, they cannot support your weight. This is because your force is acting on a small area. When you increase the number of paper cups and add the cardboard layers, your force acts on a larger area. You are spreading out the area that your force is acting on, so the cups are able to hold you up!

**STEAM CONNECTION:** Physics is a science that helps us understand what happens when forces act on things. Engineers use physics when they design structures so that they are strong and safe for us to use.

# BUILD AN EARTHQUAKE SHAKE TABLE

**DIFFICULTY LEVEL:** EASY

**TIME:** 15 MINUTES

## MATERIALS

- 2 (8.5-by-11-inch) pieces of cardboard
- 2 large rubber bands
- 2 tennis balls
- 12-inch ruler
- Duct tape

Engineers must understand how different forces will affect the structures they design and build. In some areas, earthquakes are common, and engineers must be sure that their structures can withstand the shaking created by these earthquakes. In this activity, you will build a shake table that can model an earthquake!

## STEPS

1. Place the two pieces of cardboard on top of each other. Slide a rubber band over each end.

2. Slide a tennis ball between the two pieces of cardboard at each end.

3. Place the ruler on one side, under the top piece of cardboard so that it overlaps the cardboard by three inches. The ruler should be **perpendicular** to the rubber bands.

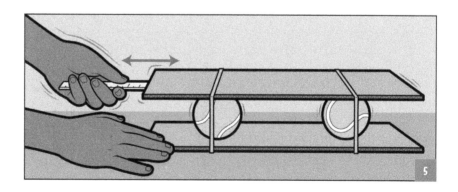

4. Secure the ruler with some duct tape.

5. Use one hand to hold the bottom piece of cardboard steady, and use your other hand to move the ruler back and forth. You're creating an earthquake!

**HOWS & WHYS:** During an earthquake, the ground moves and shakes. When structures are built in earthquake zones, engineers must be sure that they can stay standing after an earthquake. Engineers make small models of their designs and use shake tables to create a fake earthquake.

The shake table in this activity uses cardboard separated by tennis balls. The rubber bands keep the cardboard from completely falling off, and the tennis balls allow a quick back-and-forth shaking motion that behaves just like a real-life earthquake!

**⬤🅣🅔🅐⬤ CONNECTION: This activity uses creativity and art to create a shake table that acts like the ground would during an earthquake.**

# BUILD A WASTEWATER TREATMENT FACILITY

**DIFFICULTY LEVEL:** EASY

**TIME:** 30 MINUTES (PLUS 12 TO 24 HOURS WAIT TIME)

## MATERIALS

- 1 pair of gloves
- Garden spade
- Dirt
- 3 (clear or white, any size) disposable cups
- 1 piece of toilet paper
- Water
- Spoon
- Mesh sieve
- **Flocculant** (optional; pool maintenance supply)
- 1 drop of chlorine bleach

Have you ever wondered what happens after you flush the toilet? In urban areas, all **wastewater** is treated in wastewater treatment facilities. In this activity, you will create your own treatment facility!

 **Caution:** Be careful when using the flocculant and bleach. Always use gloves when using these chemicals, and ask an adult for help.

## STEPS

1. Put on gloves, and then use your spade to add some dirt to the first cup.

2. Rip the toilet paper into small pieces, and add them to the cup.

3. Fill the rest of the cup up with water, and mix well with the spoon. This is the wastewater.

4. Pour the mixture over the sieve into the second (empty) cup.

5. *Optional* Add half a capful of flocculant to the filtered mixture.

6. Mix with a spoon and let sit for 12 to 24 hours.

7. After 12 to 24 hours, look at the cup. The water should be mostly clear with all the dirt settled at the bottom.

8. Pour the clear water into the third cup. Be careful not to pour any of the dirt into the new cup!

9. Add one drop of chlorine bleach to the water and mix it. Now the wastewater is treated!

‹‹continued››

**HOWS & WHYS:** When we take a shower, do laundry, brush our teeth, or flush our toilets, that wastewater all goes somewhere. Civil engineers design wastewater treatment facilities that clean wastewater to make it safe enough to release back into the environment.

When you mixed the toilet paper, dirt, and water, you had an example of what wastewater might look like. The first step of wastewater treatment uses a screen (like your sieve) to remove large particles like sticks and debris. Next, any other particles in the water will gradually sink to the bottom. Civil engineers use flocculants to speed up this process. Flocculants make all the particles in the water clump together until they become so heavy that they sink to the bottom of the water. Next, naturally occurring bacteria in the wastewater works to break down any harmful things that may be in the water. Lastly, chlorine is added to the water to disinfect it and reduce any bad smells.

**⬤①⑤Ⓐ⬤ CONNECTION:** This activity uses science to understand how the flocculant causes particles to clump together and sink to the bottom. Also, sieves are useful tools that allow small particles to pass through but block larger particles.

# BUILD A WRECKING BALL

**DIFFICULTY LEVEL:** EASY

**TIME:** 25 MINUTES

## MATERIALS

- Building blocks (any type)
- Doorway
- Tape
- 1 key ring
- 1 large ball, like a soccer ball or a basketball
- 1 plastic shopping bag
- Yarn or twine

Sometimes when construction engineers want to build new things, they have to break down the old structures that were there before. An easy way to do this is to use a wrecking ball. In this activity, you will make your own wrecking ball!

## STEPS

1. Start by building a simple tower with blocks in the doorway.

2. Use some tape to secure a key ring to the top of the doorway.

3. Put the ball in the plastic shopping bag and tie the bag closed. Thread one end of the yarn through the handles and tie it.

4. Thread the other end of the yarn through the key ring. Adjust the height of your wrecking ball by raising or lowering the yarn.

5. While holding the yarn steady with one hand, pull the wrecking ball back with your other hand and let it go to knock down the tower!

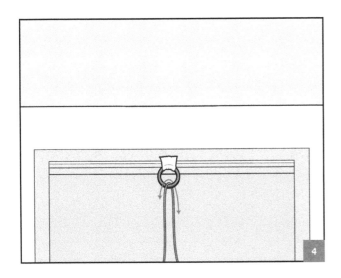

**HOWS & WHYS:** A wrecking ball is a big **pendulum**. When you pull the ball back, it lifts it higher and higher. This gives the ball more energy in the form of **gravitational potential energy**. When you release it, the ball starts to move because it is changing its **potential energy** into **kinetic energy**. The farther back you pull your wrecking ball, the higher it goes, and the more gravitational potential energy it has. This means that when you release it, it will also have more kinetic energy, and it can move faster and knock down even more blocks!

When construction engineers use wrecking balls in real life, they do the same thing. Instead of trying to force something over, they can simply pull back the wrecking ball and let it go. This way they work smarter, not harder!

**S T E A M CONNECTION:** Physics is used in this activity when the wrecking ball is pulled back and released. You are using the science of potential and kinetic energy and taking advantage of gravity to make your work easier!

# BUILD A WATER FILTER

DIFFICULTY LEVEL: EASY
TIME: 20 MINUTES

## MATERIALS

- Scissors
- 1 empty (16-ounce or larger) plastic bottle with cap
- 1 thumbtack
- 1 coffee filter
- 2 cotton balls
- Sand
- Gravel
- Muddy water

Have you heard of the water cycle? All the water on Earth is connected. We don't throw away old water or make new water because it gets reused through the water cycle. To make water safe to drink, civil engineers treat water, and a part of the water treatment process uses filters. In this activity, you will learn how to make your own filter!

 **Caution:** Thumbtacks and scissors can be very sharp. Be careful when you are using them, and ask for help from an adult!

## STEPS

1. Use the scissors to cut the plastic bottle in half.

2. Use the thumbtack to poke holes in the cap of the bottle. Poke enough holes so that water can drip through the cap.

3. Screw the cap back onto the bottle and place the top half of the bottle upside down inside the bottom half of the bottle.

4. Place the coffee filter in the top half of the bottle.

5. Add the two cotton balls on top of the coffee filter.

6. Add a one-inch layer of sand on top of the cotton balls.

7. Add a one-inch layer of gravel on top of the sand.

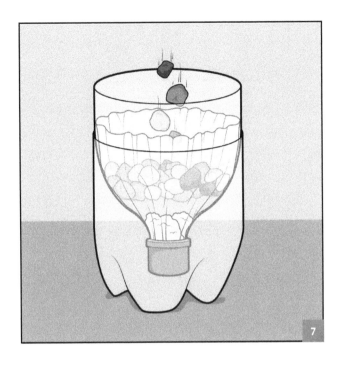

8. Slowly pour the muddy water on top of the gravel.

9. Look at the water dripping into the bottom half of the bottle. Is it muddy or clear?

**HOWS & WHYS:** Civil engineers clean and filter water at water treatment plants before the water gets to our homes. In this project, you used different types of filters to get the soil particles out of the water. As the water travels through the filter, the holes get smaller and smaller. The water goes through gravel on top, then sand, then cotton, and, finally, a coffee filter. The bottle cap full of holes helps slow the water as it goes through the filter, so large particles are filtered out on top, and smaller particles are filtered out on the bottom.

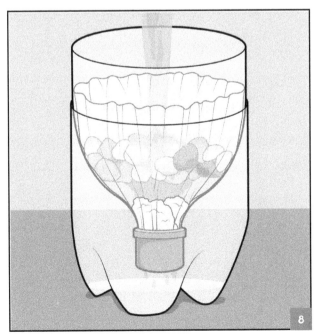

⬤TⒺⒶ⬤ CONNECTION: We use science to understand how different materials can work together to filter particles out of water. Also, we learn that the slower that dirty water moves through a filter, the cleaner it becomes!

# BUILD A WATER PRESSURE EXPERIMENT

**DIFFICULTY LEVEL:** EASY
**TIME:** 20 MINUTES

## MATERIALS

- Screwdriver
- Empty gallon plastic jug
- Duct tape
- Water

Did you know that water has different pressure depending on how deep it is? In this experiment, you will demonstrate how water pressure changes with the depth of water in a jug.

 **Caution:** You will need to use the screwdriver to poke holes in the empty jug. Screwdrivers can be sharp, so ask an adult for help!

## STEPS

1. Use a screwdriver to poke three holes into a plastic gallon jug. Be careful, and ask an adult for help! Punch one hole near the top, punch one hole near the bottom, and punch one hole in the middle. Try to line the holes up for easy observation.

2. Cover each hole with duct tape and fill the jug with water.

3. Remove the duct tape from the top hole, then the middle, and, finally, the bottom.

4. Observe how the water drains out of each hole.

**HOWS & WHYS:** As the depth of water increases, the water pressure increases. This is because as you go deeper and deeper in water, more and more water is above, increasing the pressure.

When engineers design and build dams, they must understand how much force the water will create. Engineers must understand how much water pressure is acting on the dam. The deeper the water, the greater the pressure, so dams must be able to handle the largest forces at the bottom of a dam.

**STEAM CONNECTION: This activity uses science to understand how water pressure changes with the depth of water.**

# BUILD A SOIL VOLUME EXPERIMENT

**DIFFICULTY LEVEL:** EASY
**TIME:** 25 MINUTES

## MATERIALS

- 1 empty potato chip can (or another cylinder that fits inside one of the cups)
- Small rocks (enough to fill the cylinder)
- 2 (16-ounce) disposable cups
- Moist dirt

When construction engineers are on a construction site, they move a lot of dirt around! Sometimes the same amount of dirt can have a different **volume**, depending on how much air is mixed in. In this activity, you will see how soil expands after you **excavate** it!

## STEPS

1. Fill your chip can with small rocks.

2. Fill the first cup with one inch of moist dirt.

3. Use the filled chip can to compact, or smash down, the dirt. Try to get it as tightly packed as you can!

4. Repeat steps 2 and 3 until the cup is completely full of **compacted** dirt.

5. Next, use a spoon to carefully scoop the dirt out of the first cup and into the second cup. DO NOT compact.

6. Continue scooping dirt into the second cup until it is full. How much dirt is left in the first cup?

**HOWS & WHYS:** **Native soil** is packed very tightly and doesn't have much air mixed in. The cup with the compacted dirt is like native soil. When you dig that dirt out with your spoon, it's just like when engineers excavate dirt on a construction site.

After you fill the second cup with dirt, you'll notice that the first cup still has some dirt left inside. This is because when you excavate dirt, you're mixing in air, and that makes the dirt take up more space. This increase in volume is called **expansion**.

**STEAM CONNECTION:** This activity uses science to understand how the volume of soil can change by mixing in air. Construction engineers also use math when they use expansion factors to predict how much the native soil will expand once it is excavated.

# BUILD A ROAD

**DIFFICULTY LEVEL:** MEDIUM
**TIME:** 20 MINUTES, PLUS OVERNIGHT TO DRY

## MATERIALS

- Shoebox
- Dirt
- Gravel/stones
- Sand
- Medium-size mixing bowl
- White glue

Roads help us move around our communities and go from one place to another. You might know what a road looks like on top, but have you ever wondered what it looks like under the surface? This project will help you understand the different parts of a road.

## STEPS

1. Fill the shoebox with just enough dirt to cover the entire bottom. This will be the **subgrade** of your road.

2. Get your subgrade ready by squishing it into the bottom of the box. When we pack the dirt like this, we call it compaction.

3. Add a layer of gravel on top of the subgrade. Pour the stones in from the top, and try not to move the subgrade that you have already compacted. This is the **base layer** of your road.

4. Pour some sand into the mixing bowl, and add glue until it is easy to mix. If your mixture is clumpy, add more glue. If it is runny, add more sand.

5. Pour the sand-and-glue mix on top of your base layer. This is the **wearing course** of your road.

6. Let your road dry overnight.

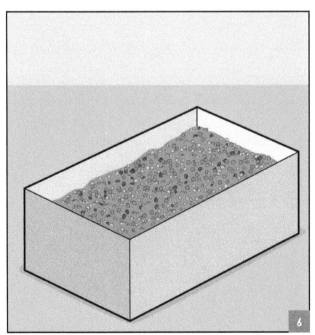

**HOWS & WHYS:** Roads are built on top of dirt that is already at the construction site. When this dirt is compacted, it becomes the subgrade of the road. Compaction makes sure that the road doesn't sink in certain areas after cars and trucks drive on it.

Roads have many layers that help make them stronger. A stone layer as the base adds strength while still letting water, like rain, pass through. Different types of concrete are used on top, like asphalt concrete or Portland cement concrete, that acts like glue to hold smaller rocks and sand together. These concrete layers are what we drive on. The top layer is called a wearing course because that is the part that wears away over time.

⬤**T**⬤**A**⬤ **CONNECTION:** Roads require the use of both engineering and math. Engineers use something called a mix design to figure out how much concrete (in this case, glue) to mix with stones and sand to build a strong, long-lasting road. When you decide how much sand and glue to use in your mix, that's your own mix design!

# BUILD A PULLEY

**DIFFICULTY LEVEL:** MEDIUM
**TIME:** 15 MINUTES

## MATERIALS

- Low-temperature glue gun and glue sticks
- 2 (14-ounce) empty cans
- 1 trifold poster board
- 2 tennis balls
- 1 small bucket or pail with handle
- Twine
- 1 carabiner

When a new building is under construction, sometimes workers need to lift heavy materials from the ground to the top of the building. One way of doing this is to use a pulley system. Pulley systems can make it easier to lift things. In this project, you will create your own pulley.

 **Caution:** Glue guns can get very hot (even low-temperature ones). Have an adult help when you are using a glue gun.

## STEPS

1. Use the glue gun to glue two cans to the poster board side by side.

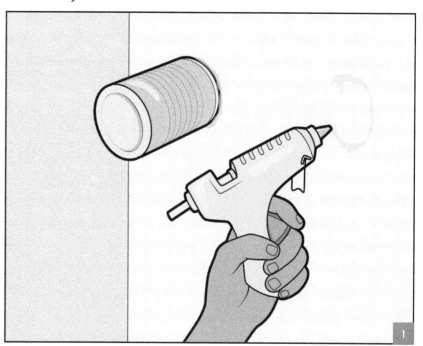

2. Add the tennis balls to the bucket.

3. Try picking up the bucket. Think about how heavy it feels as you hold it.

4. Drape the twine over one of the cans, and tie one end of the twine to the handle of the bucket.

5. Pull down on the other end of the twine, and watch the bucket as it goes up. Does it feel heavier, lighter, or just the same?

6. Now add some more pulleys to the system. Untie or cut off the twine from the bucket.

7. Tie one end of the twine around one of the cans.

8. Make a U shape with the twine, and hold it in place while you drape the other end of the twine over the second can.

9. Clip the bucket handle to the carabiner and clip this to the bottom of the U.

10. Pull down on the free end of the twine, and watch as the bucket goes up. Does it feel heavier, lighter, or just the same?

«continued»

**HOWS & WHYS:** Pulleys are a type of simple machine and a great example of how technology can make our jobs easier. As you add more pulleys to the system, the **load** becomes easier and easier to lift.

⬤⒯⒡Ⓐ⬤ CONNECTION: Engineers use physics to design simple machines, like pulley systems, and new technology to make their jobs easier.

# DESIGN A SUBDIVISION

**DIFFICULTY LEVEL:** MEDIUM

**TIME:** 1 HOUR

## MATERIALS

- 1 (22-by-28-inch) poster board
- Pencil
- Colored pencils
- Paint

Subdivisions can be found in suburban communities, where areas of land are divided into **lots** to build new homes. Civil engineers plan and design these subdivisions to meet the needs of these new communities, while following any local and regional laws. For this project, you will plan and design your own subdivision, just like engineers do in real life!

## STEPS

### PART 1:

1. You need to create 18 lots. There is one major road that allows access to the subdivision, and this road runs parallel to the bottom of the poster board. Create a roadway that connects to this major road. The roads must be perpendicular to each other and each lot must have access to a road.

2. Use a pencil to draw your roads and lots so that all the space on one side of the poster board is used. Try to have the lots about the same size.

3. Use colored pencils and paint to complete your **conceptual design**.

### PART 2:

Imagine that the mayor has added a new rule saying that for all new subdivisions, 25 percent of the area must be green space, like a park. On the other side of your poster board, design space for 18 lots again, but this time, 25 percent of the space will be a community park. Each lot as well as the park must be accessible by a road.

4. Draw a rectangle that takes up one-quarter of the poster board to make room for the park.

5. Decide where you want the roads to go, making sure that everyone has road access.

6. Divide the remaining area evenly to make room for 18 lots.

7. Use colored pencils and paint to complete and decorate your design.

8. Show off your design to your family for **public input** on your plans!

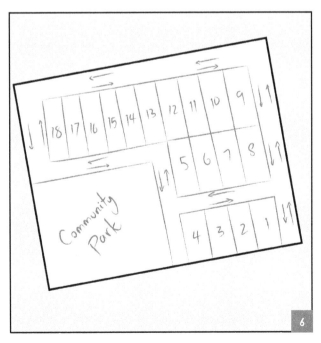

**HOWS & WHYS:** When civil engineers plan and design subdivisions, they decide the best way to split the large area into smaller lots for homes. Each home must have access to a roadway that lets them travel in and out, and the engineers must decide where everything is placed to avoid wasted space.

Sometimes there are special rules for the design. For this project, you needed to create a design that had room for 18 lots and room for a community park. Engineers have to follow all of the rules for the area that they are designing for.

≪continued≫

When designing new roads, engineers try to make sure that drivers can easily see any oncoming traffic at an intersection. The road in your subdivision is perpendicular to the major road so drivers can see oncoming traffic and safely leave the subdivision.

**STEAM CONNECTION:** When planning and designing subdivisions, engineers must use creativity and art to design beautiful and functional communities. You also use math in this activity to divide an area into 18 equal lots and when you design your community park to take up 25 percent of the space.

# DESIGN AND BUILD A LEVEE

**DIFFICULTY LEVEL:** MEDIUM

**TIME:** 45 MINUTES

## MATERIALS

- Duct tape
- Craft sticks
- 1 quart-size plastic bag
- Plastic container, at least 6 inches deep and less than 7 inches wide
- Cotton balls
- 1 cup of sand
- 1 cup of gravel
- Sponge
- Dirt
- Water
- Measuring tape

Communities that are close to water are at risk for flooding after severe storms. Levees can help protect these communities by creating a barrier between the water source and the community. For this project, you will design and build your own levee!

## STEPS

1. Use duct tape to attach craft sticks to the inside of each end of the quart-size bag. This will be your levee.

2. Decide which side of the container will be your river and which will be your city. Place the levee in the middle of the container, and select materials from the list to secure the levee in place. Remember, you need to protect the city from the river that is overflowing its banks. This is your design, so you get to decide how and with what you will attach the levee to the inside of the container to keep the city completely dry!

3. Now add five inches of water to the river side of the container. Did your levee work? If not, how can you improve your design?

4. Tweak your design until your levee works!

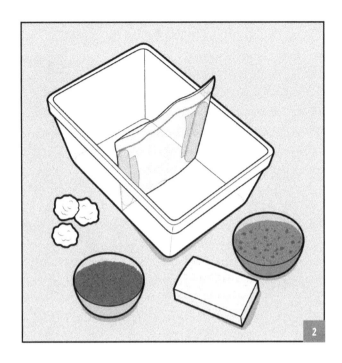

**HOWS & WHYS:** Real levees must be both tall and wide enough to prevent flooding. For this project, you needed to design a levee that was at least five inches high and able to keep water in one half of the plastic tub while the other half stayed dry. You had to choose the materials that were best suited to keeping the water on one side of your container. The water will flow wherever there is a weak point: around the sides or even under the levee. An important part of engineering is coming up with a design, testing that design, and improving it. It's okay if your first design doesn't work. As a future engineer, you must be able to understand why your design didn't work and figure out how to improve it.

**⬤①③④⬤ CONNECTION:** This activity uses art and creativity to select materials and come up with a design for the levee. You must also use science to understand that water pressure is highest at the bottom of the container, so you must be sure that the bottom of the levee is strong enough to block the water that is trying to push through.

# BUILD A WHEELBARROW

**DIFFICULTY LEVEL:** MEDIUM
**TIME:** 30 MINUTES

## MATERIALS

- 1 (6-inch) bowl
- Pencil
- Cardboard sheets (enough to make six 6-inch circles)
- Scissors
- Low-temperature glue gun and glue sticks
- 1 cardboard box
- 2 broom handles
- 1 plunger stick (take off the plunger end)

You may have seen a wheelbarrow or two being used on a construction site. Wheelbarrows are another type of simple machine that makes it easier to lift and carry heavy loads. It might be difficult to carry a big bag of rocks from one place to another, but it's easy if you use a wheelbarrow!

 **Caution:** Glue guns can get very hot (even low-temperature ones). Have an adult help when you are using a glue gun. Scissors can be extremely sharp. Be careful using them, and ask an adult for help if you need to.

## STEPS

1. Use the bowl to trace six circles on the cardboard sheets. Then use scissors to cut the circles out.

2. In the middle of each circle, cut a hole big enough for the plunger stick to fit through.

3. Use the glue gun to glue three circles together. Try to stack them as neatly as possible since this will be one of your wheels.

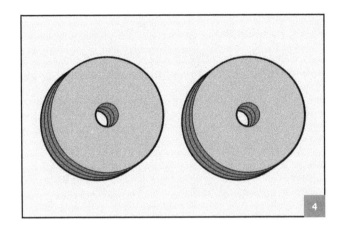

4. Repeat step 3 for the other three circles. Now you should have two wheels.

5. Cut four holes near the top of the cardboard box, two on each side. The holes should be large enough for the broom handles to go through, and each hole should line up with one on the other side.

6. Slide each broom handle through the holes at the top of the cardboard box. The handles should run parallel to the long side of the box.

7. Cut two holes near the bottom of your cardboard box, one on each side. Push the plunger stick through, leaving about 2 inches outside the box on each end. This is the **axle**.

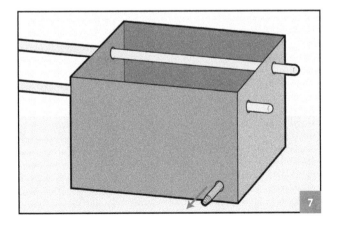

≪continued≫

8. Push each of your cardboard wheels onto each end of the axle. Your wheelbarrow is complete! Test it by adding a load!

**HOWS & WHYS:** A wheelbarrow is a type of lever that has three major parts: a **pivot**, a load, and **effort**. A seesaw is a type of lever that has the pivot in the middle, a load on one end, and the applied effort on the other end. When you play on a seesaw, you can easily lift your friend on one end by pushing down at the opposite end.

In a wheelbarrow, the pivot is on one end (the wheels), the load is in the middle (the box, in this case), and the applied effort is on the other end. The farther away the effort is from the pivot, the less force is needed to lift the load. Also, the closer the load is to the pivot, the less force is needed to lift the load.

**STEAM CONNECTION: Simple machines use physics to make it easier for us to move things. Physics teaches us about forces and helps us work smarter, not harder!**

# BUILD A RAILROAD

DIFFICULTY LEVEL: MEDIUM
TIME: 30 MINUTES

## MATERIALS

- 7 (0.5- to 0.75-inch-wide) craft sticks
- Low-temperature glue gun and glue sticks
- 12 half-inch wooden craft cubes
- Gravel or stones
- 1 adult-size shoebox

Railroads help move people and supplies from one place to another. There are three major pieces needed to build a railroad: rails, ties, and ballast, meaning something heavy. Trains travel on rails. Ties keep rails together. Ballast holds everything in place.

 **Caution:** Glue guns can get very hot (even low-temperature ones). Let an adult help when you are using a glue gun.

## STEPS

1. Place three craft sticks on a flat surface and keep them about a craft stick's length apart from each other. These craft sticks will be the **ties**.

2. Use the glue gun to glue two wooden cubes together. These cubes will be the **tie plates** that connect the rails to the ties. Repeat five more times until you have six pairs of cubes.

3. Use the glue gun to stick a tie plate to one end of one of the ties. Glue another tie plate to the other end of the tie.

4. Add tie plates to the other two ties you laid out. Now you're ready to add the rail!

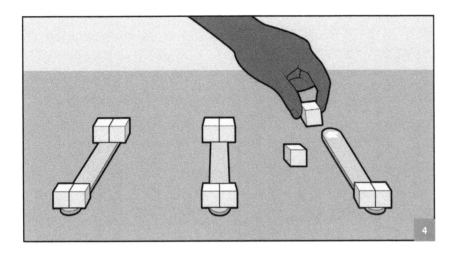

5. Place a craft stick on its side, and glue it on each end to a tie plate to create your first rail. Be sure to leave room on the tie plate for your next piece of rail!

6. Glue another craft stick next to the last piece of rail and onto the next tie plate.

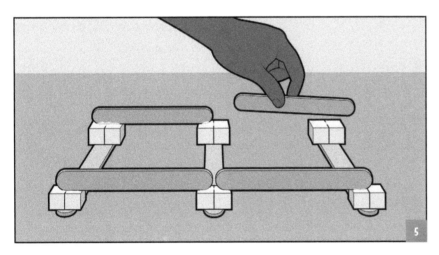

7. Repeat steps 5 and 6 to add rail to the other side of your ties. Congratulations, you have built a **skeleton track**!

<<continued>>

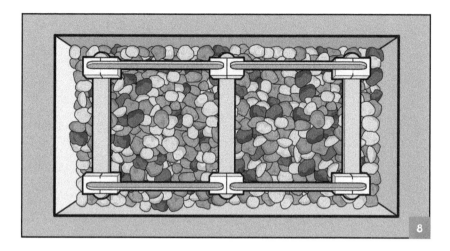

8. Pour some stones or gravel into a shoebox big enough for your track to fit in. Place the skeleton track on top. Push the skeleton track down gently into the rock to make sure everything is secure.

9. Now you can take your railroad with you to show everybody what you built!

**HOWS & WHYS:** First, you put the ties and the rails together on the "ground" since it is easier to build track on a flat surface. This is called a skeleton track because it looks just like a skeleton before adding muscles and skin!

Next, the ballast is added to keep the ties and rails in place. It is important to use rough and pointy rocks for the ballast because they lock together and stay secure in place. Ballast also helps keep water away from the rails since there is enough space between the rocks for rain to drain through.

**CONNECTION:** A science called geology helps engineers choose the best type of rocks for ballast. In this project, you also used math to make sure that the rails were straight and that the ties were at right angles to the rails.

# BUILD A TRAIN CAR

## MATERIALS

- Pencil
- 1 small (3-by-8-inch) piece of cardboard
- 1 large bottle cap (like a sports drink cap)
- Scissors
- 1 small bottle cap (like a water bottle cap)
- Low-temperature glue gun and glue sticks
- Thumbtack
- 1 small (3-by-6-inch) gift box
- 2 (0.25-by-5-inch) wood dowels

Have you ever looked at a train car or locomotive and wondered how they stayed on the rails? Have you ever heard loud screeching when a train passes by? This project will help you understand how trains work and how they can move without falling off of the rails!

 **Caution:** Glue guns can get very hot (even low temperature ones). Let an adult help when you are using a glue gun. Thumbtacks and scissors are extremely sharp, so be careful when using them for this project.

## STEPS

1. Trace four circles onto the cardboard piece using the large bottle cap. Cut them out.

2. Trace eight circles onto the cardboard piece using the small bottle cap. Cut them out.

3. Use the glue gun to stick two small circles in the middle of a large circle. Repeat for the other three large circles. These will be your wheels.

4. Use the thumbtack to poke a hole toward the front of the gift box, near the bottom. Remove the thumbtack, and push the pencil through the hole to widen it. Repeat on the other side of the box.

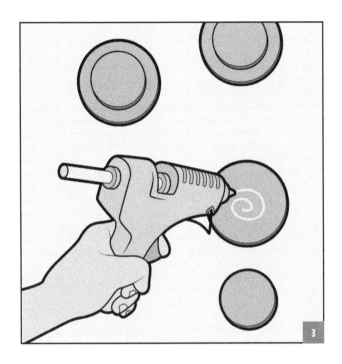

5. Push one of the dowels through the holes you just made. This is your front axle.

6. Repeat steps 4 and 5 for the back of the gift box. This is your rear axle.

**HOWS & WHYS:** Trains can move large, heavy loads easier than trucks can, so construction materials are often transported long distances using trains. Unlike cars or trucks that drive on roads, trains ride on rails. The wheels have to be specially designed to travel on rails. Just like in this project, a real train car wheel has two parts. The small circles rest on the rail, and the large circles help to stabilize the wheel on the rail. The axles spin with the wheels and move the train car forward.

If a rail is bent or if a train is traveling too fast on a curve, the larger part of the wheel, the **flange**, helps to keep the train on the tracks. Real train wheels are also tapered, and that helps trains travel in curves, too.

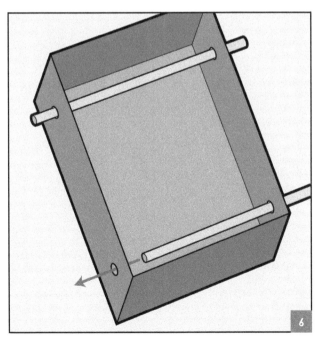

‹‹continued››

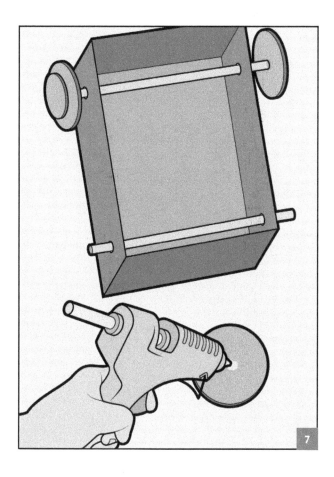

7. Hot glue the wheels to the front and rear axles on the gift box. The larger circles should be on the inside, and the smaller circles should be on the outside.

**STEAM CONNECTION:** Math is used to measure the train car. The axles have to be wide enough so that the wheels can travel on the rails. If the axles are too wide or too short, the train car won't be able to move on the rails!v

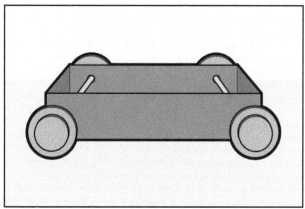

# BUILD A SHAPE STRENGTH EXPERIMENT

**DIFFICULTY LEVEL:** MEDIUM

**TIME:** 30 MINUTES

## MATERIALS

- Modeling clay
- Toothpicks
- 1 small book (or weight)

When engineers design structures, there are many shapes that they can choose from. In this project, you will compare a square and a triangle to see which shape is stronger!

## STEPS

1. Make four small balls out of modeling clay.

2. Use the clay balls to connect the corners of the toothpicks to form a square.

3. Pick up the square and push on one of the corners. What happens?

4. Remove one toothpick and one ball and reshape into a triangle.

5. Pick up the triangle and push on one of the corners. What happens?

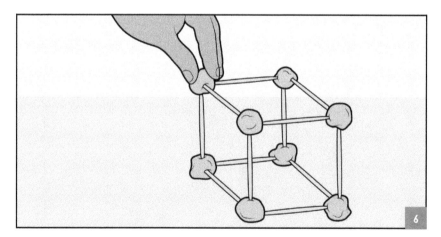

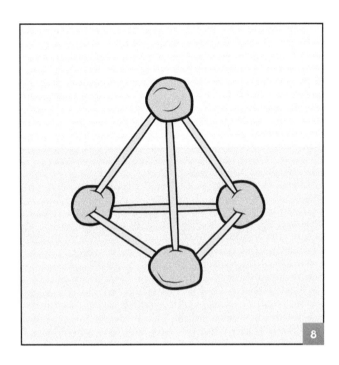

6. Use balls of modeling clay and toothpicks to make two squares. Connect the squares together with more toothpicks to make a cube.

7. Place a small book or weight on top of the cube. What happens?

8. Use balls of modeling clay and toothpicks to make another triangle. Use three more toothpicks and one small ball to make a **tetrahedron**.

9. Add toothpicks and clay to add extra tetrahedrons. Keep going until you have six tetrahedrons connected.

10. Place the same book on top of the tetrahedrons. What happens?

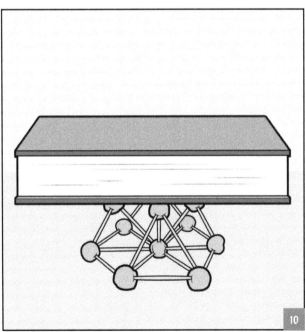

‹‹continued››

**HOWS & WHYS:** When you push on the corner of the square, it collapses. When you push on the corner of the triangle, it doesn't move. This happens because the angle between two sides of the triangle is fixed based on the length of the opposite side. Squares can change their shape because the angles can change without having to change the length of their sides.

The cube collapses when you place the book on top because the cube is made up of connected squares. The tetrahedrons can support the book because they are made using triangles.

When engineers design structures like **trusses**, a special type of framework support, they use triangles since those shapes won't collapse like we saw with the squares.

⬤🅣🅕🅐🅚 CONNECTION: **This activity uses math to understand how the angles in a triangle relate to the length of their sides. Math shows us that triangles cannot change their angles without changing the length of the sides.**

# BUILD A GEOGRID EXPERIMENT

## MATERIALS

- Permanent marker
- 2 (4-inch-diameter) cylinders open on both ends (such as short PVC pipe)
- 3 coffee filters (or wire mesh)
- Scissors
- Wet sand
- 1 empty chip can full of rocks (or any other heavy cylinder that fits inside your 4-inch-wide cylinder)
- Load (a few bricks or heavy books)

When construction engineers build structures on site, sometimes the native soil isn't strong enough to support a load. Engineers use geogrids to add strength to soils. For this project, you will see how two identical soil samples perform with and without geogrids!

 **Caution:** Scissors can be very sharp. Be careful when you are using them, and ask for help from an adult!

## STEPS

1. Trace four circles with your marker on the coffee filters or mesh using the inside of your 4-inch cylinders.

2. Use your scissors to cut the circles out.

3. Label your cylinders "A" and "B."

4. Fill each cylinder with one inch of wet sand.

5. Use your heavy chip can to compact the sand. Try to get it as tightly packed as you can!

6. Place one of the mesh or coffee filter circles inside cylinder B only.

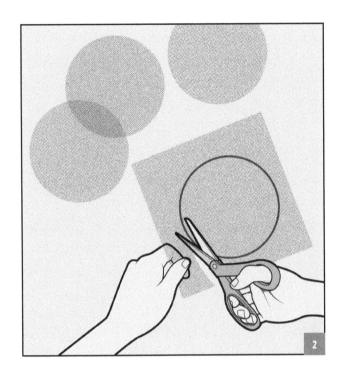

7. Repeat steps 4 to 6 three more times, until you have four layers of sand. Remember to add a mesh or coffee filter circle to cylinder B only after every layer of sand.

8. Add a final one-inch layer of sand to each container, and compact it.

9. Carefully slide the cylinders up off the sand, like you do when making a sandcastle. You will now have two towers of sand, one with geogrids and one without.

10. Slowly add your load to the sand tower from cylinder A. How much load can it carry before it **fails**?

<<continued>>

11. Slowly add your load to the sand tower from cylinder B. How much load can it carry before it fails?

**HOWS & WHYS:** For this project, you created two identical samples, except one has a geogrid (the coffee filters) and the other does not. When you add the load to the sample with no geogrid, it falls apart. When you add the load to the sample with a geogrid, it is able to carry that load.

The geogrid in this project holds the sand together so that it doesn't crumble. This allows it to carry a larger load than it would be able to without the geogrid **reinforcement**.

**STEAM CONNECTION:** This project uses physics to understand how a sample will react when a load is added. You're also using the scientific method when you compare two samples that have only one difference.

# BUILD AN UNDERDRAIN SYSTEM

**DIFFICULTY LEVEL:** MEDIUM
**TIME:** 40 MINUTES

## MATERIALS

- Scissors
- 1 empty macaroni-and-cheese box (or a similar size)
- Clear tape
- 1 jumbo straw
- Pen
- 1 or 2 coffee filters
- Dirt
- Water

Have you ever wondered where water goes after a big storm if you can't see any drainpipes or channels? Sometimes civil engineers use underdrains to move water away from structures like buildings or roads. These underdrains are hidden underground, so you can't see them, but they're always working! For this project, you will learn how to build your own!

 **Caution:** Scissors can be extremely sharp. Be careful when using them, and ask an adult for help.

## STEPS

1. Use scissors to cut off the front of the box. Secure the corners with tape.

2. Cut a small V on one side of the jumbo straw to reveal a diamond-shaped hole. Repeat this cut along the length of the straw, with one inch between each hole.

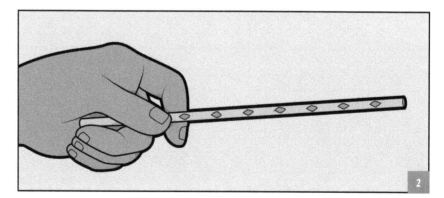

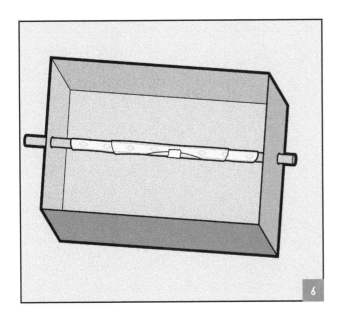

3. Trace the hole of the jumbo straw onto the lower part of one end of the box. Use a pen to poke a hole in the middle of the circle.

4. Trace the hole of the jumbo straw again onto the upper part of the other end of the box. Use the pen to poke a hole in the middle of the circle.

5. Cut a coffee filter so that it will wrap around the entire straw just once, covering all the holes. Use tape to secure the filter paper to the straw.

6. Push the jumbo straw through the holes on each end of the box.

7. Fill the box to the top with dirt. Shake the box from side to side to make sure that there are no empty spaces, or **voids**.

8. Take the box outside, and slowly pour water over the middle of the box (above the jumbo straw). What happens?

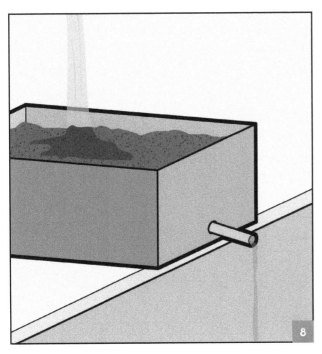

<<continued>>

**HOWS & WHYS:** Water can make structures weak, so engineers work very hard to keep water away from things they build, like buildings and roads. Underdrains are a great way to move excess water away from structures.

Engineers install these underdrains at an angle, just like the straw in this project, so that gravity will move the water through the drains. No pumps or other equipment are needed! Engineers use a special type of filter fabric called **geotextiles** to wrap the underdrains. Geotextiles keep the underdrains clean and free from **sediment** that can clog underdrains and stop them from working how they should.

⬤**T**🅖🅐⬤ CONNECTION: **You use science when you place underdrains at an angle because you are using gravity to make the water flow on its own, without a pump. Good drainage is also an important part of projects that engineers design and build.**

# BUILD A SILT FENCE

DIFFICULTY LEVEL: MEDIUM

TIME: 20 MINUTES

## MATERIALS

- A spot outside that you're allowed to dig in
- A digging tool (a pencil will work)
- 6 standard craft sticks
- Clear tape
- 1 pack of coffee filters
- Muddy water
- Measuring tape

Have you ever noticed a short black fence that surrounds a site while it is under construction? This is called a silt fence, and it stops mud and dirty water from leaving the construction site. In this activity, you will build your own silt fence so you can understand how it works!

## STEPS

1. Find a two-foot-long spot outside where you can dig a small, slightly curved trench.

2. To dig your trench, take your digging tool or pencil and drag it across the ground to make a slightly curved line two feet long.

3. Keep dragging your tool along this line until it is about a half inch wide and a half inch deep.

4. Push one of your craft sticks into the ground inside one end of your trench. It should go about one inch into the ground.

5. Repeat this for the other five craft sticks, placing one every five inches along the trench.

6. Use tape to stick the coffee filters to the trench side of each craft stick. Use as many coffee filters as you need to create a continuous fence of coffee filters. Let the bottom of the filters drape into the trench.

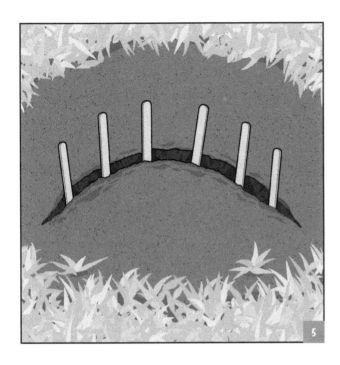

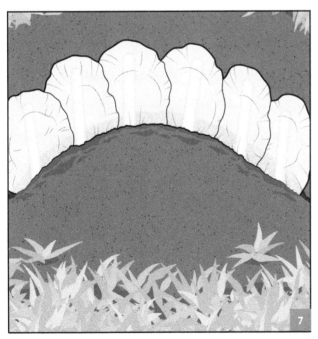

7. Fill the trench back up with dirt. Your silt fence is complete!

8. Slowly pour some muddy water toward the middle of the fence. What happens?

**HOWS & WHYS:** Trees and grass naturally stop soil erosion. During construction, when trees or grass that cover the ground are removed, the ground becomes exposed. Erosion happens when exposed soil or dirt is washed away, and it can flow into our rivers and streams. Construction engineers use silt fences to keep this sediment from getting into our waterways. After the project is complete, engineers replant trees and grass to cover the ground, and remove the silt fence.

‹‹continued››

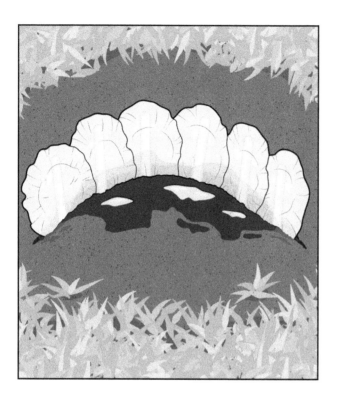

⬡ⓉⒺⒶ⬡ CONNECTION: When you space your craft sticks for your silt fence, you are using math to make sure that the sticks are evenly spaced. Also, you use science when you use a special filter to stop the soil particles from escaping.

# DESIGN AND BUILD AN EARTHQUAKE-PROOF TOWER

**DIFFICULTY LEVEL:** MEDIUM
**TIME:** 30 MINUTES

## MATERIALS

- 1 (8.5-by-11-inch) piece of cardstock
- Modeling clay
- 50 plastic coffee stirrers
- 2 binder clips

When engineers design buildings that are in earthquake zones, they must be sure that those buildings will not fall during or after an earthquake. In this activity, you will design a building that can withstand an earthquake!

## STEPS

1. Place the cardstock on a flat surface. Make a square using balls of modeling clay and coffee stirrers. Stick the clay of your square to the cardstock. This will be the base of your building.

2. Use the stirrers and clay to make a cube on top of the base.

3. Add a stirrer above each top corner of the cube, and connect them with one piece of clay. Your first building is complete!

4. Carefully move your building and place it on top of an earthquake shake table. (See page 20 to make your own.)

5. Use binder clips to secure the cardstock to the cardboard.

6. Hold the bottom of the shake table with one hand, and hold the ruler with the other. Start shaking!

7. Did your building stay up or collapse? You can do a few things to improve the design.

8. Try adding more triangular shapes.

AWESOME CONSTRUCTION ACTIVITIES FOR KIDS

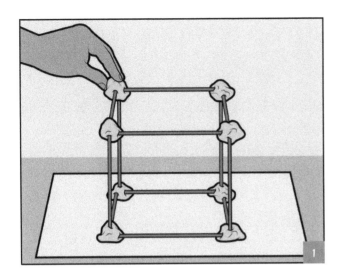

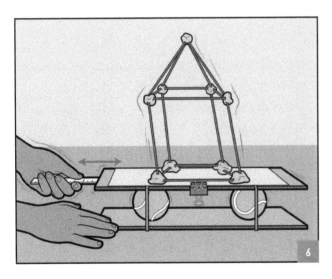

9. Try making a wider base to make your tower sturdier.

10. Try adding crossbracing by dividing a square into two triangles with a coffee stirrer to make your building sturdier.

11. After improving your design, test it again! Keep going until you have a tower that can withstand an earthquake!

**HOWS & WHYS:** Engineers create small models of their designs and test them on shake tables to understand how the building will act during and after an earthquake. Engineers have found that wider bases, triangular shapes, and crossbracing can make buildings sturdier in an earthquake. A wide base will make the building sturdier and prevent it from tipping over. Triangles are stronger than rectangles or squares, so adding triangles will prevent the building from collapsing.

**CONNECTION:** This project uses science to know that when the table shakes, it creates forces that act on the tower. This activity also uses math to choose the strongest shape to hold up the tower.

# DESIGN AND BUILD A CLOVERLEAF INTERCHANGE

**DIFFICULTY LEVEL:**
CHALLENGING
**TIME:** 1 HOUR

## MATERIALS

- Scissors
- 8 (8.5-by-11-inch) black cardstock sheets
- Glue
- 1 (22-by-28-inch) poster board
- 3 cardboard toilet paper tubes
- Chalk

Have you ever taken a road trip with your family and noticed huge roads that travel on top of each other and in different directions? Those roads form interchanges. In this activity, you will design a special type of interchange: a **cloverleaf**!

 **Caution:** Scissors can be extremely sharp. Be careful when using them, and ask an adult for help.

## STEPS

1. Cut two pieces of cardstock lengthwise into three-inch-wide strips. Glue enough strips end to end to create two roads that are long enough to form a "+" and go from end to end of the poster board.

2. Glue one road down the middle of the poster board.

3. Cut one toilet paper tube in half. Glue one half on each side of the road, equal distance apart. These are the **bridge piers**.

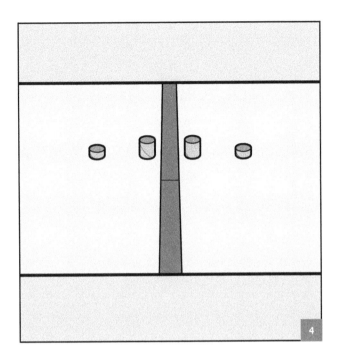

4. Cut the other toilet paper tubes into quarters. Glue one quarter to each side of the road, past the bridge piers, equal distance apart.

5. Glue the other road perpendicular to the first, on top of the bridge piers. Now there are two roads in place, one on top of the other. This is a **grade-separated crossing**.

6. Draw the direction of traffic with chalk. In the United States, cars drive on the right side of the road. Draw arrows to show where the cars should be going.

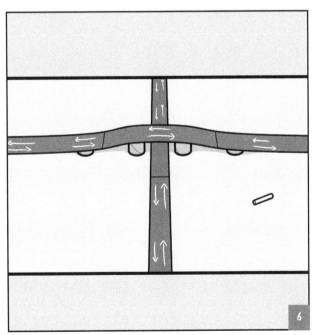

&lt;&lt;continued&gt;&gt;

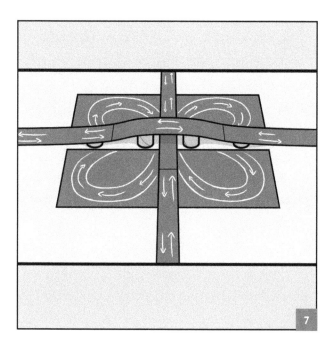

7. Place one piece of cardstock on each corner of the grade-separated crossing. Draw a loop on each piece of paper. Draw arrows on the loops that match up to the ones you already drew on the other roads.

8. Cut out the loops and glue each loop to the road. Glue the loop end that is connected to the lower road onto the poster board. Glue the loop end that is connected to the top road onto the top road. These are the **ramps**.

9. Slide one toilet-paper-tube quarter under the raised portion of each loop for support. These loops form the cloverleaf.

10. Use the rest of the cardstock to make four new roads. Connect these to each end of the two original roads to form a diamond.

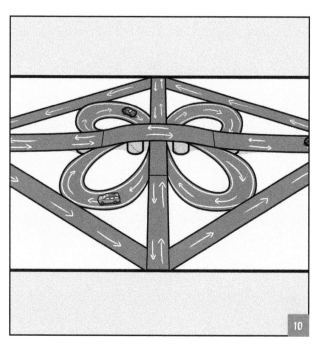

**HOWS & WHYS:** Cars usually travel at low speeds in neighborhoods where stop signs and traffic lights control the flow of traffic. For longer trips, people want to travel faster, but at higher speeds, it is harder to stop safely. Also, even if it wasn't harder, there would be lots of delays if there were lots of stops.

On highways and freeways, civil engineers keep people safe by designing interchanges like the cloverleaf. Grade separations allow one road to cross over another so people don't have to stop to let other cars through.

**⚫⬤⬤⬤⬤ CONNECTION: This activity uses math to measure the width of the roads and to design the curves of the ramps. The finished cloverleaf also looks like a real cloverleaf, so the roads can be your own work of art!**

# BUILD A REINFORCED CONCRETE SLAB

**DIFFICULTY LEVEL:**
CHALLENGING
**TIME:** 1 HOUR (PLUS
4 HOURS WAIT TIME)

## MATERIALS

- 1 wire hanger
- Fishing line or thread
- Wire cutters (optional)
- Fast-setting concrete mix
- 3 shoeboxes (or any other rectangular box)
- Water
- Garden spade
- 2 bricks or pavers

Engineers love to use concrete because it is extremely strong and durable. Sometimes concrete is not strong enough on its own, though, so engineers add steel to it. Concrete with steel is called **reinforced concrete**, and in this project, you'll make your own to understand how important it is!

 **Caution:** Have an adult help with this activity and wear protective gloves. Wire hangers and wire cutters can be extremely sharp. Working with fast-setting concrete can also be dangerous.

## STEPS

1. Have an adult help unwind your wire hanger into a straight piece.

2. Bend the wire into three equal sections. Tie fishing line or thread around the wire to keep the sections parallel to each other, or, if you have wire cutters, cut the wire into three equal pieces.

3. Pour enough dry concrete mix into one shoebox to cover the bottom of the other two shoeboxes.

4. Slowly add water to the concrete. Mix it well with the spade until the concrete looks like pancake mix with rocks in it.

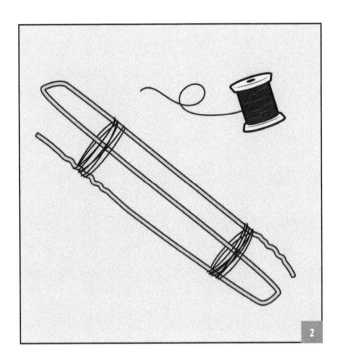

5. Put a little concrete into a second shoebox. Place the wire you bent or cut on top of the concrete. Cover the wire with concrete until it is an inch thick. Smooth the concrete out with the back of the spade. This will be a concrete **slab**.

6. Pour an inch of concrete into the third shoebox. Use the spade to smooth out the top. Label this second concrete slab as "no wire."

7. Wash the spade before the concrete hardens.

8. Let the concrete **cure** on a flat surface for four hours.

9. Peel the shoeboxes off the concrete.

10. Place a brick under each end of the "no wire" slab. Get a grown-up to stomp in the middle of the concrete slab. What happened?

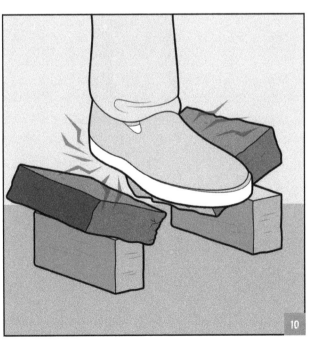

≪continued≫

11. Repeat step 10 with the "wire" slab. What happened?

**HOWS & WHYS:** Concrete is extremely strong in **compression**, or forces that push together, but not as strong in **tension**, or forces that pull apart.

Putting a concrete slab on the bricks acts like a bridge. When you push down on the bridge, the top of the bridge is in compression, and the bottom is in tension. It's almost like when you lie down to do crunches. When you crunch, the muscles in your belly crunch together, but your back stretches out.

The first concrete slab breaks. This is because the concrete on the bottom is very weak in tension. The reinforced concrete slab, however, cracks near the bottom, but stays in one piece. This is because you added steel, which is strong in tension.

**⬤ⓉⒼⒶ⬤ CONNECTION: This activity uses physics to understand which part of the bridge is in tension and which part is in compression.**

# BUILD A SELF-SUPPORTING BRIDGE

**DIFFICULTY LEVEL:**
CHALLENGING
**TIME:** 25 MINUTES

## MATERIALS

- 18 craft sticks
- Marker

Have you ever heard of the famous artist Leonardo da Vinci? Did you know he made lots of other things besides art? One of his famous creations is a self-supporting bridge. In this activity, you will learn how to build a bridge that can carry a load, using only sticks! You will build this bridge by weaving, so pay close attention to the illustrations and stick numbers to keep things simple. Just take one step at a time!

## STEPS

1. Start by numbering your sticks 1 through 18 with a marker.

2. Place stick 1 down on the table, then place sticks 2 and 3 on top of stick 1.

3. Add stick 4 on top of sticks 2 and 3.

4. Carefully lift stick 1, and weave sticks 5 and 6 under stick 1 and over stick 4.

5. Slide stick 7 under sticks 5 and 6.

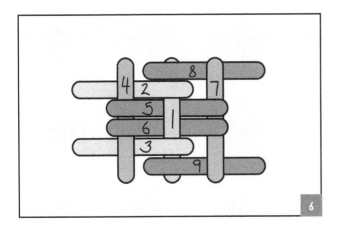

6. Slide sticks 8 and 9 under each end of stick 7 and over each end of stick 1.

7. Place sticks 10 and 11 on top of stick 7.

8. Place stick 12 under stick 8, over sticks 10 and 11, and under stick 9.

9. Slide stick 13 under sticks 10 and 11.

10. Carefully lift stick 13, and weave sticks 14 and 15 under stick 13 and over stick 12.

11. Slide stick 16 under sticks 14 and 15.

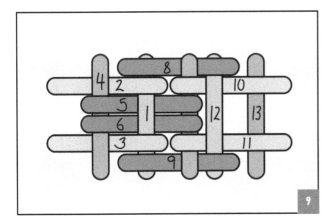

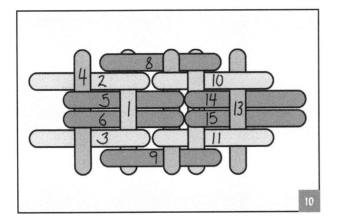

&lt;&lt;continued&gt;&gt;

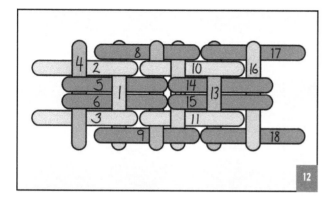

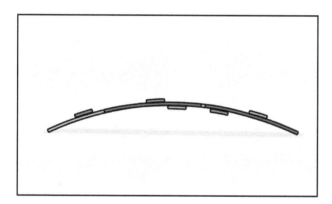

**12.** Slide sticks 17 and 18 under each end of stick 16 and over each end of stick 13. Congrats! You did it!

**HOWS & WHYS:** This bridge is held together by friction and gravity. Leonardo da Vinci originally designed this as an emergency bridge to be used during war. A bridge that doesn't need any fasteners or adhesives would be easy to build in a battle and easy to remove so that the enemy couldn't use it!

**CONNECTION:** This bridge was designed using physics. The original designer, Leonardo da Vinci, was a great artist. He used his creativity to design a bridge that was both practical and beautiful.

# BUILD AN AUGER

## MATERIALS

- Scissors
- 1 empty (20-ounce) plastic bottle
- Pencil
- 1 (8.5-by-11-inch) cardstock sheet
- Tape
- Thumbtack
- Bowl of dry cereal or popcorn

In ancient times, the Archimedes's screw was invented to move water up from a lower level to a higher level. This design is still used today, and civil engineers use a type of Archimedes's screw called an **auger** to move dirt on a construction site. In this activity, you will build your own auger!

 **Caution:** Thumbtacks and scissors can be very sharp. Be careful when you are using them, and ask for help from an adult!

## STEPS

1. Very carefully, cut off the bottom of the bottle and cut a triangular hole near the top of the bottle.

2. Use the cut edge of your bottle to trace a circle onto the cardstock. Cut out the circle along the inside of your traced lines, so that it's slightly smaller and will fit snugly inside the bottle.

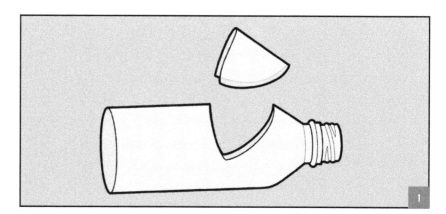

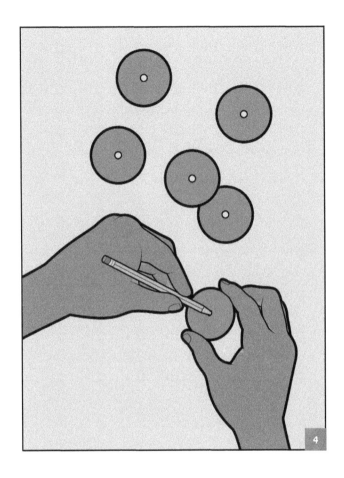

3. Cut five more circles based on the first one, for a total of 6 circles.

4. Use the point of your pencil to poke a hole in the middle of each circle. Thread the circles onto the pencil, point-end first, so that the holes are just big enough to fit on the pencil.

5. Take the circles off of the pencil. Use your scissors to cut a straight line from the edge of each circle to its center hole.

6. Slide the six circles back onto the pencil and space them evenly.

7. Tape the cut area of each circle to the next to make a spiral. Tape each end of the spiral to each end the pencil.

8. Push your pencil with the spiral into the plastic bottle, with the eraser side facing the bottle cap.

9. Caefully push the thumbtack through the bottle cap and into the eraser.

‹‹continued››

**10.** Place your auger diagonally into the bowl of cereal. Make sure the cereal can enter the triangular hole that you cut out. Spin the pencil on the free end, and watch as the cereal is lifted through the bottle and out on the other end!

**HOWS & WHYS:** An auger looks like a large drill, and construction engineers use augers to move dirt. It makes it easier whether you have to dig small holes, like a hole for a fence post, or large holes, like a huge underground tunnel.

As you spin the auger, the cereal gradually moves up the tube on the spiral and falls out of the top. This is very useful if you are digging a hole, since the dirt keeps moving up and out of the hole. Civil engineers also use augers in paving machines to push and spread asphalt out over the road.

**STEAM CONNECTION:** This activity uses math to measure and cut the circles. It also uses science to understand how to move the cereal up on the auger by twisting.

# BUILD A FLOATING STRUCTURE

**DIFFICULTY LEVEL:**
CHALLENGING
**TIME:** 45 MINUTES

## MATERIALS

- ➔ 10 craft sticks
- ➔ Low-temperature glue gun and glue sticks
- ➔ Scissors
- ➔ Thread

Have you ever seen an "impossible" table that seems to float without legs? In this activity, you will build your own floating structure. It's not magic; it's engineering!

**Caution:** Glue guns can get very hot (even low-temperature ones). Have an adult help when you are using a glue gun. Scissors can be very sharp. Be careful when you are using them, and ask for help from an adult!

## STEPS

1. Make a square using four craft sticks. Hot glue the corners together to secure.

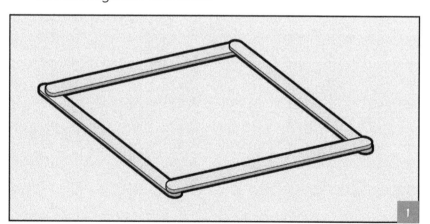

2. Repeat step 1 to make another square.

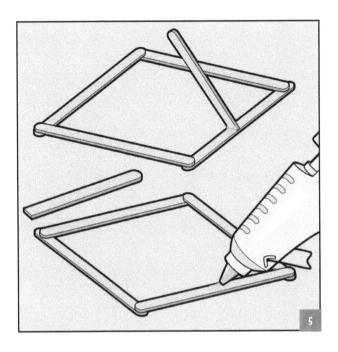

3. Take one craft stick and measure three-quarters of the length of the stick. At the three-quarter mark, cut the stick at a 45-degree angle.

4. Hot glue the cut end of your craft stick to the middle of one side of the first square.

5. Repeat steps 3 and 4 to cut another craft stick, and hot glue it to the second square.

6. Cut four pieces of thread that are the same length as an uncut craft stick.

7. Stack the two squares on top of each other with the angled craft sticks facing inward. The angled craft sticks should be facing each other from opposite sides.

8. Hot glue the four pieces of thread to each corner of the two squares. Your squares should now be connected at the corners.

9. Hold the top square up so that the threads are tight. Measure the distance between the angled craft sticks, and cut a piece of thread that length.

10. Let the top square rest. Glue the last piece of thread to each end of the angled craft sticks.

11. Pull the top square up and make sure all threads are tight. It floats!

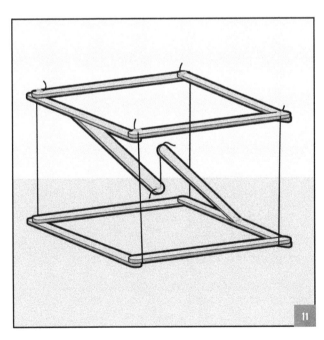

«continued»

**HOWS & WHYS:** Civil engineers make sure that the structures that they design are in **equilibrium**, which means that all the forces balance out. When we first look at this floating structure, it seems impossible that it could stand without collapsing. When you look closer, you can see that all the forces balance out.

Try holding a piece of thread in your hands. When you pull the thread in opposite directions, the thread becomes tight and is in tension. If you try pushing the thread together, it just folds and gathers together. For a thread to be tight, it has to be in tension.

In the floating structure, the threads are all tight, meaning that they are all in tension. Something is pulling the thread from either side. The squares are pulling against each other, and you can see that tension in the threads at each of the four corners. But what is making those squares pull against each other? It's the craft sticks in the middle and the thread that's in tension. The sticks are also pulling on each other, balancing all the forces.

⬡①Ⓣ🅕🅐⬡ CONNECTION: There is a lot of math in this activity! It is very important to measure the thread and the angle of the cut craft sticks correctly for this activity to work. Engineering and science teach us how to balance forces.

### Part III

# PUTTING IT ALL TOGETHER

**The projects in this book focus on different** kinds of civil engineering and construction activities and why they are so important to us. Civil engineers create the designs, or instructions, for construction engineers to follow. Construction engineers must know when to follow instructions and when to change the design if something doesn't work the way it was planned. In order to complete these projects, you needed to understand how to follow instructions, but you also needed to understand how to change things to make a design work even better.

Think about the engineering design process and how it relates to each project: ask, imagine, plan, create, and improve. With each project in this book, you gained experience that teaches you how to become better at solving problems by using the engineering design process. This is the same experience that civil and construction engineers gain in real life!

# I'M A CONSTRUCTION ENGINEER!

Construction engineers must use science, technology, engineering, art, and math to bring designs to life. Each activity in the book showed the STEAM connection to show just how important all of these subjects are when designing and building infrastructure.

As you worked through this book, you designed and built different projects that covered every type of civil engineering. Projects like the earthquake-proof tower show the importance of structural engineering. Geotechnical engineers use science to look closely at what type of soil is in place, as in the soil-testing activity, so that they can design strong foundations. Transportation engineers use math and art to design roads and highways like the cloverleaf project. Environmental engineers protect the environment and use technology to clean the wastewater that leaves our homes in wastewater treatment facilities like the one you built yourself. Hydraulic engineers use both science and math to study the flow of water, just like in the water pressure experiment. And, of course, construction engineers bring designs to life, just like you did in all these activities!

# CONSTRUCTION ALL AROUND YOU

A big part of being an engineer is being able to adapt to change. When you needed to design a subdivision, you got to see that sometimes engineers have to change designs to meet certain rules, even if those designs originally worked. In the real world, engineers have lots of challenges, such as changes in design requirements or from a new rule or law that was added after the project started. Engineers have to figure out how to get the job done even when there are new challenges thrown their way.

Each project had a Hows and Whys section that explained how these projects related to real life. These activities are all really cool, but what's even more interesting is learning how these projects work. When you built a road you used common materials like sand and glue to understand how the top layer of a road works. You got to use (and smash!) real concrete and saw how steel makes concrete stronger when you made reinforced concrete. Every project explained the small details about construction that lots of people don't even consider. Think about building an underdrain: Every detail, from the sloping pipe to the covered holes, is carefully put into place to make sure that water can drain away from structures.

Construction is really all around you in both seen and unseen ways. You'd be surprised by what you notice when you start paying closer attention!

## BUILD ON!

The next time you drive down the street, think about the engineering that went into deciding how and where to build that road. The next time you pass a construction site, think about what those engineers are doing to make sure that those buildings stand tall for years to come. The next time you drink water or take a shower, think about how engineers clean and treat the water that enters or leaves your home.

Think about these engineering and construction aspects in everyday life—things you see around you all the time. Never stop wondering why. Never stop asking questions. Never stop looking for solutions. If you keep learning and keep building, one day, you, too, can contribute to the engineering wonders of the world!

The skyscraper's the limit.

# GLOSSARY

**AUGER:** A tool used to drill holes in the ground

**AXLE:** A rod that passes through the center of a wheel and allows rotation

**BASE LAYER:** The layer of compacted crushed rock under a road

**BRIDGE PIER:** A bridge support

**CLOVERLEAF:** A highway interchange that looks like a clover leaf

**COMPACTED:** Packed tightly

**COMPRESSION:** Force that pushes together

**CONCEPTUAL DESIGN:** A basic drawing that shows the first phase of a design

**CURE:** The chemical process that involves the hardening of concrete

**EFFORT:** Force that you exert

**EQUILIBRIUM:** A state of balance

**EXCAVATE:** To dig

**EXPANSION:** Swelling of soil when excavated and mixed with air

**EXPANSION FACTOR (OR SWELL FACTOR):** Used to determine how much excavated soil will expand

**FAIL:** No longer able to carry a load

**FLANGE:** Edge of a wheel that is larger than the rest of the wheel

**FLOCCULANT:** An additive that causes the clumping of particles

**FORCE:** A push or pull on an object

**GEOTEXTILES:** Permeable fabrics that can filter, separate, or drain

**GRADE-SEPARATED CROSSING:** Roadways that cross each other at different levels: overpass (bridge) or underpass (tunnel)

**GRAVITATIONAL POTENTIAL ENERGY:** The energy an object possesses due to its distance from the Earth and the gravitational attraction to the Earth

**INFRASTRUCTURE:** Anything built or man-made that supports modern life

**KINETIC ENERGY:** The energy an object possesses due to its motion

**LOAD:** The force exerted on an object

**LOAM:** Soil with almost equal amounts of sand, silt, and clay

**LOTS:** Divided areas of land

**NATIVE SOIL:** Soil that naturally exists before construction or development

**PENDULUM:** A body suspended from a fixed point so that it can swing back and forth under the influence of gravity

**PERPENDICULAR:** Crossing another line at a right angle (90°)

**PIVOT:** The point at which something turns

**POTENTIAL ENERGY:** The energy an object possesses due to its position

**PRESSURE:** The amount of force exerted per area

**PUBLIC INPUT:** Feedback from the general public

**RAMP:** A short road that lets vehicles enter or exit a highway

**REINFORCED CONCRETE:** Concrete with wire or steel added in to increase its strength

**REINFORCEMENT:** The act of strengthening something

**SEDIMENT:** Matter that settles to the bottom of a liquid

**SILT:** A component of soil with particles larger than clay but smaller than sand

**SKELETON TRACK:** Railroad track before adding ballast

**SLAB:** A flat horizontal piece of concrete

**SUBGRADE:** The native material under a road

**TENSION:** Force that pulls apart

**TETRAHEDRON:** A polygon with four triangular faces

**TIES:** Support for rails laid perpendicular to the rails

**TIE PLATES:** Steel plates used between rails and ties

**TRUSS:** A framework used to support roofs, bridges, and other structures

**VOID:** The space between soil particles made up of air or water

**VOLUME:** The amount of space taken up by a substance

**WASTEWATER:** Contaminated water

**WEARING COURSE:** The top layer of a road

# RESOURCES

**Visit these websites for fun civil and construction engineering activities:**

**ASCEville.org**
- Civil engineering resources for teachers and parents

**DiscoverE.org/discover-engineering**
- Engineering resources for parents of students interested in engineering

**KenkenKikki.jp/e_index.html**
- Construction equipment resources for students

**PBS.org/wgbh/buildingbig/abt_chall .html**
- Fun civil engineering challenges for students

# INDEX

# ABOUT THE AUTHOR

**Akyiaa Morrison** is a Professional Engineer and the founder and president of her own engineering consulting firm. Morrison grew up with a passion for construction and earned her BS and MS in civil engineering. She has extensive experience in road and railroad construction, asset management, and capital planning. Morrison is also a proud homeschooling mom of two, and in her free time, she enjoys teaching students ages 3 to 18 all about engineering.

Printed in the USA
CPSIA information can be obtained
at www.ICGtesting.com
CBHW050337310524
9306CB00011B/146